TABLE OF CONTENTS

LORD CHARLES CORNWALLIS: A STUDY IN STRATEGIC LEADERSHIP FAILURE

"So far as active campaigning was concerned, Yorktown ended the war. Both Greene and Washington maintained their armies in position near New York and Charleston for nearly two years more, but the only fighting that occurred was some minor skirmishing in the South. Cornwallis' defeat led to the overthrow of the British cabinet and the formation of a new government that decided the war in America was lost. With some success, Britain devoted its energies to trying to salvage what it could in the West Indies and in India. The independence for which Americans had fought thus virtually became a reality when Cornwallis' command marched out of its breached defenses at Yorktown"[1]

"In 1781 Lord Charles Cornwallis effectively ended the American Revolution by surrendering at Yorktown."[2] Not only did Cornwallis lose at Yorktown, but in doing so, he lost the American colonies to the British Empire. The career of Lord Charles Cornwallis as a strategic leader is filled with intriguing questions. Why did Cornwallis surrender at Yorktown when a large British fleet under Sir Henry Clinton, that could well have meant victory for the British, was in route from New York? Did he not understand that a victory at Yorktown over Washington and Rochambeau's combined land and naval forces could have broken the will of the Americans and French to continue the prosecution of the war? Finally, how is it possible that the man largely responsible for the loss of the American colonies to the British Empire went on to become a British military and political "superstar"? The answers to these questions can be found by studying Cornwallis' development as a practitioner of the strategic leadership competencies as defined in the U.S. Army War College's (USAWC) Strategic Leadership Primer.

The purpose of this paper is to examine Lord Charles Cornwallis' early "failures" as a practitioner of the strategic leadership competencies that ultimately led to his defeat at Yorktown and the loss of the American colonies to the British Empire. Using the framework of the competencies overlaid on Lord Cornwallis' American Revolutionary War career this paper will illustrate that the development of great strategic leaders can be a dangerous learning process fraught with costly errors in judgment, particularly when operating within the fog of war as Cornwallis did while in command of the Southern Theater from 1780-1781. The relevance of this examination is that it provides a vehicle from which developing senior leaders can gain insight into the strategic leadership competencies by studying the early strategic failures of one of the British Empire's greatest military officers and statesmen.

This paper is not intended to be an in depth biography of the life of Lord Charles Cornwallis, nor is it an all-inclusive analysis of the attributes and qualities required of a great strategic leader. It is designed to study (through the lens of the strategic leadership competencies) some of Cornwallis' more notable failures during the Revolutionary War to demonstrate how he learned, sometimes with a resistance born of arrogance, to methodically assimilate the characteristics and skills that would one day make him a superlative strategic leader.

The examination of Cornwallis' early failures as a practitioner of the strategic leadership competencies begins with an overview of the competencies and their components. Following this a series of historical vignettes and anecdotes is provided to examine Cornwallis' early years as a developing leader, his pre-command years in the American Revolution, and his actions in both the Carolinas and Yorktown campaigns. A synopsis of Cornwallis' career after Yorktown is presented, with history's assessment of him as a strategic leader, that illustrates he truly internalized the competencies as he became more senior. Finally, a conclusion is provided.

THE STRATEGIC LEADERSHIP COMPETENCIES: AN OVERVIEW

> "Strategic-leader competencies fall under the three rubrics of conceptual, technical and interpersonal. These competencies are supported by a broad and rich frame of reference developed throughout the leader's life, and this enables the leader to deal with tremendously complex issues and events."[3]

The USAWC's Strategic Leadership Primer states that leadership at the highest level is practiced in an environment characterized by volatility, uncertainty, complexity, and ambiguity (VUCA). "The strategic leader must be an expert, not only in his/her own domain of warfighting and leading large military organizations, but also in the bureaucratic and political environment of the nation's decision-making process."[4] Therefore, it is incumbent upon the strategic leader, not only to achieve this mastery of the strategic environment, but to exercise those *strategic-leader competencies* that will foster accomplishment of their vision within that complex environment.[5] The Strategic Leadership Primer asserts that the competencies are derived from a leader's lifetime worth of education, training or experience. Specifically, it defines the major categories of leadership competencies as conceptual, technical and interpersonal.[6]

Conceptual competency includes the clear thinking skills required of leaders who will deal in extremely complex environments. The ability to deal with competing issues, prioritize risks and understand second- and third-order effects of decisions are all integral to the conceptual competency. Components of the conceptual competency include frame of reference development (a "map" of the strategic world based on a lifetime of experience), problem management (managing problems towards the desired outcome and selecting the best solution from among competing courses of action), and envisioning the future (capability to formulate and articulate strategic aims).[7]

Technical competency requires the "understanding of organizational systems, an appreciation of functional relationships outside the organization, and knowledge of the broader political and social systems within which the organization operates."[8] The components of the technical competency are systems understanding (how one's organization operates in the broad international arena), joint and combined relationships (how to operate in a multicultural environment), and political and social competence (the ability to function as a member of a policy formulation team and to understand the relationship between stated and operating values).[9]

Interpersonal competency is the strategic leader's ability to successfully interact with those people, organizations and agencies both internal and external to his sphere of influence. The components of the interpersonal competency include consensus building (gaining commitment by being persuasive through effective reasoning), negotiation (communicating a clear position on an issue while conveying a willingness to compromise), and communication (internally and externally in a brief, clear, and persuasive manner).[10]

It should be pointed out that applying a set of competencies refined in the information age to an eighteenth century warrior/statesman might seem inconsequential. The eighteenth century strategic leader obviously did not enjoy the near instant interaction with seniors, peers and subordinates that communications advances give them today. As a result decisions made by them (especially when under duress) may seem less than optimal, or even ludicrous, given our ability to armchair quarterback some two hundred years later. It is my assertion, however, that the conceptual, technical and interpersonal skills discussed above are, in fact, timeless attributes required of strategic leaders in any age. After all, in their most basic form the competencies are nothing more than the ability of senior leaders to synergize thinking skills, interpersonal dynamics, and the ability to communicate and negotiate in a coherent problem solving process.

CORNWALLIS' EARLY LEADERSHIP DEVELOPMENT

"He had his baptism of fire and served his apprenticeship. Eaton had made the boy a man, and the Seven Year's War had made the man a soldier. Already, before his twenty-fourth birthday, he had developed qualities of self-reliance, determination, physical endurance, moral and physical courage - resources he would need when he went to America."[11]

Lord Charles Cornwallis was born in 1738, the eldest son of a titled and highly respected family. Cornwallis' grandfather was a baron under King Charles, his father was the first Earl Cornwallis, and his uncle was the Archbishop of Canterbury. Cornwallis' mother was the daughter of Lord Townshend and a niece of Robert Walpole, former Prime Minister of England.[12]

Cornwallis' formal education took place at Eaton academy and Clare College, Cambridge. Although most young men of Cornwallis' station went on to Oxford (and useless lives of leisure) he possessed a strong sense of duty and instead chose the military as a career, purchasing an ensign's commission in 1756. Since England had no military academies at the time Cornwallis was tutored by a Prussian officer and then trained at the military academy at Turin, Italy. Shortly after his enrollment, however, the Seven Year's War broke out in Europe and Cornwallis decided to leave Turin and fight for the Empire. During this conflict Cornwallis distinguished himself, first as a staff officer and then, as the Lieutenant Colonel of the 12th Foot, in combat at Minden, Kirch Donkern, and Lutterburg.[13]

In 1762, Cornwallis' father died and he became the second earl of Cornwallis. His sense of duty demanded that he return home and take his father's seat in the House of Lords. His abilities and connections there led to his becoming the Aide-de-Camp to the King. King George III showed a fondness for Cornwallis, as they were much alike in the areas of character and temperament. During his time as a member of Parliament, Cornwallis consistently voted against harsh legislation aimed at the colonists in America, such as the 1766 Declaratory Act, even when in a distinct minority among his peers. Although sympathetic to the grievances of the Americans, Cornwallis put his sense of duty to King and Empire first as he accepted a commission, in 1775, as Major General, and volunteered for service in the colonies. [14]

Measured in terms of military and political experience Cornwallis should have been the outstanding British General in the American Revolution.[15] His success as a military officer thus far in his career, his familiarity with the inner workings of the British government, and a first hand knowledge and, presumably understanding of the King's policies in particular would all lead one to believe that his success as a strategic leader would have been pre-ordained. However, while that at this stage of his development Cornwallis had a firm grasp on the tactical and operational levels of conflict, he had simply not been put in a position where he alone was responsible for formulating, advising on and executing strategic level policies. Although Cornwallis had internalized the twin codes of duty and honor that constituted the code of the great generals and statesmen of England's past he had not yet learned, and therefore not mastered, the "integrative thinking skills required of strategic leaders."[16]

PRE-COMMAND YEARS IN AMERICA

Cornwallis arrived in America in time for the first expedition against Charleston in June 1776. This operation, led by Sir Henry Clinton, was poorly planned and executed, ending in a miserable failure.[17] As a result of the Charleston debacle "the earl could not have been impressed by Clinton's abilities as a leader"[18] Charlestown was the initial interaction of Clinton and Cornwallis, laying the foundation of squabbling and jealously between the two for the rest of the war, eventually playing an important part in Cornwallis' surrender at Yorktown.

From Charleston, Cornwallis proceeded north to take part in the Battle of Long Island in August 1776 where "Lord Cornwallis and a flying wedge of 4500 men"[19] helped outflank the Americans and forced them from New York. After the action at Long Island he was involved in several successful engagements around New York. In November 1776, while pursuing the Continental Army across New Jersey, on orders from General Howe, British Commander-in-Chief, Cornwallis halted his forces at New Brunswick, thus allowing Washington to escape into Pennsylvania. Halting Cornwallis' aggressive pursuit, which might have ended in the defeat of the American army, set the stage for the attacks by Washington on troops under Cornwallis at Trenton and Princeton in early 1777.[20] Although ordered to stop the pursuit of the Americans, Cornwallis was humiliated (and in some circles judged at fault) by Washington's escape and subsequent victories at Trenton and Princeton. Typical of Cornwallis' offensive minded spirit he vowed that, "from that time forward this British general would never again be criticized for lack of energy."[21] At the battles of Brandywine in September 1777, where Cornwallis' troops broke the Continental Army's back, and again at Monmouth in June 1778, where "he fought his last major battle under another officer's leadership,"[22] Cornwallis consistently "demonstrated that he was a field commander of considerable ability."[23]

Throughout his pre-command years in America Cornwallis honed his skills as an extremely competent operational commander. His chances to develop his strategic leadership competencies during this period were limited, but did exist. Cornwallis displayed a glimpse of his budding conceptual skills when he proved he was more cognizant than General Howe regarding the possible opportunity the destruction of the American army before they escaped into Pennsylvania presented. On the negative side, Cornwallis' inability to try to get along with Clinton (his superior officer) demonstrated a weakness in his interpersonal competency, that would prove disastrous when, upon Howe's resignation in 1778, Clinton became British Commander-in-Chief. The following quote aptly highlights Cornwallis' continued refinement of his tactical and operational skills, while at the same time hinting at his overall lack in development of the strategic leadership competencies during the pre-command years in the colonies. "In his first 18 months in America, the earl had distinguished himself in subordinate roles and proved he was an able and colorful field commander."[24]

THE CAROLINAS CAMPAIGN

In 1780, the British strategy for winning the war changed from victory in the north to "a systematic, purposeful effort to restore the king's authority in the southern colonies."[25] "The basic concept was to regain military control of some one major colony, restore full civil government, and then expand both control and government in a step-by-step operation conducted behind a slowly advancing screen of British regulars."[26] It was anticipated by Lord Germain, who was running the war from his ministry in London, that this strategy would "bring out the loyalists in such numbers that the army would have little fighting to do and would act primarily in support of Tory operations."[27] To initiate this new strategy Sir Henry Clinton, with Cornwallis as his second in command, seized Charleston, S.C. in August 1780. The loss of more than 5500 American troops under General Benjamin Lincoln at Chalreston was "the most severe reversal suffered by an American army during the war."[28]

After the capture of Charleston, Clinton returned to New York (fearing an American/French attack), leaving Cornwallis in command of the Southern Theater to conduct what the British thought would be a simple mopping up campaign to subordinate the Carolinas to British control. It was anticipated that Cornwallis would simply march through the Carolinas, easily defeat any resistance from the patriots and then firmly entrench the loyalists in control of the local governments of the liberated areas.[29]

Now that Cornwallis was in command of the Southern Theater it was up to him to execute the British strategy that would energize the southern loyalists who, the British believed, far outnumbered the patriots, and thus bring the entire populace back into the fold.[30] Cornwallis' actions over the next fourteen months demonstrate that he simply did not have an adequate understanding of the conceptual, technical, and interpersonal skills required to ensure strategic victory in the south. His inability to integrate the strategic leadership competencies can be seen in four strategic miscalculations. These, formulated early while in command in the Carolinas, t eventually led to his defeat at Yorktown. First, Cornwallis believed that if he could defeat the American army in the south in a single major battle the entire south would capitulate and return to British rule. Second, he misjudged the commitment of the loyalists who he, like Germain, expected to flock by the thousands in support of their king as he marched through the Carolinas. Third, Cornwallis underestimated the strength, determination and fighting ability of Nathanael Greene, and partisan guerrilla bands led by men such as Francis Marion, Thomas Sumter and

Andrew Pickens. Finally, Cornwallis consistently exhibited an unwillingness to maintain proper contact with or to follow the directives and guidance of his Commander-in-Chief, Sir Henry Clinton.[31]

The major battles of the Carolina campaign illustrate that Cornwallis was continuously trying to engage the patriots in the culminating battle that would end the war. The patriots, however, preferred a war of attrition combined with the effective use of guerilla tactics. The campaign began with Cornwallis' complete rout of the Americans under Horatio Gates at the Battle of Camden in August 1780. Unfortunately for Cornwallis, this result caused George Washington to send Nathanael Greene to replace Gates in October 1780. That same month, patriot frontier riflemen defeated a strong British raiding party, under Patrick Ferguson at the battle of King's Mountain. Next, in January 1781, a force of Americans under Dan Morgan, met and annihilated a large British raiding party led by Banastre Tarleton at the Battle of Cowpens. Then, in March 1781, Cornwallis won a costly victory over Nathanael Greene at the Battle of Guilford Courthouse. Although Cornwallis technically won this final major battle in the Carolinas campaign, his heavy losses and incessant harassing by patriot partisan bands highlighted the flaws in his culminating battle theory and forced him to retreat to British-held Wilmington, N.C. and ultimately to Virginia.[32] By retreating to Wilmington and then Virginia Cornwallis gave up all that he had gained as a result of initial impressive victories at Charleston and Camden.

The expected loyalist support never materialized in the numbers that Cornwallis had counted on. He was extremely "disappointed in the response of our people in South Carolina and Georgia. They flocked in, they took the oath, but they were not reliable."[33] Cornwallis' lack of understanding of this problem at the strategic level demonstrates his shortfall as a conceptual thinker. Initially following a British victory, the loyalists would join the British only to be abandoned by Cornwallis as he continued to move on in search of the final battle. As soon as British troops were gone, the partisan bands would descend on the loyalists and exact terrible retribution from them. As time went by, the loyalists found it safer to leave the south or, at the very least remain neutral. Cornwallis never looked at this problem holistically and simply dismissed the loyalists as unreliable and therefore not worth the investment in time and resources.[34] This shortsightedness ensured that the British strategy for bringing the south back into the fold was doomed to failure.

Cornwallis did not comprehend that, in Nathanael Greene and his regular and partisan patriot soldiers, he was engaging extremely competent opponents. Patriot resistance was proving more stubborn than expected, and Greene's unorthodox practice of fighting a battle (often losing), then retreating and dividing his forces, while at the same time harassing the

British troops through the use of guerilla warfare was extremely frustrating for Cornwallis.[35] He seriously underestimated Greene's ability to see the strategic value to the overall war effort of continuously draining the resources of the British forces in the South. One of Cornwallis' officers summed up the contribution of Greene and his partisans by remarking that, "the more he is beaten, the farther he advances in the end. He has been indefatigable in collecting troops and leading them to be defeated."[36]

Greene's tactics, and Cornwallis' lack of appreciation of their effectiveness at the strategic level, cost him the Carolinas campaign and eventually played a large part in driving him to seek refuge at Yorktown. Although Cornwallis claimed technical victories whenever he personally led troops into battle against the Americans, his victories were hollow. "It had been a disastrous campaign for the British general, despite all his claims of victory. He had been out-generalled and out maneuvered."[37] Cornwallis' divestiture of the Carolinas and his movement into Virginia is proof that he misunderstood his responsibility for executing the British policy in the South and underscores his lack of strategic competency regarding the part his actions had in the overall "step-by-step" scheme of operations.

When Sir Henry Clinton had left Cornwallis in command in the south it was with the understanding that he would remain in constant communication with the Commander-in-Chief in New York. Clinton fully expected Cornwallis to eventually return the bulk of his forces to New York where Clinton believed the outcome of the war would be realized. Cornwallis formed his own strategy that suggested the seat of the war should shift to Virginia. At the time, and without Clinton's knowledge, he was in direct communication with the British Ministry in London pleading his case.[38] With Lord Germain's approval, Cornwallis headed to Yorktown in the summer of 1781 to assume a strong position on the Virginia coast to be close to British logistical support from the sea. Clinton had no choice but to accede to Lord Germain's wishes and grudgingly accepted the new strategy.[39] During this time there was little direct communication between Cornwallis and Clinton. The historically bad feelings between the two was, therefore, aggravated and was partly responsible for the lack of support Cornwallis would require when surrounded by American and French forces at Yorktown.[40]

Throughout the Carolinas campaign, and into the early phases of the Yorktown campaign, Cornwallis was certainly at fault for not keeping his superior informed of his actions and plans. Cornwallis' low opinion of Clinton as a commander, and his direct communication with London, clearly undermined the unity of command effort that was essential to British victory.[41] This shortfall on Cornwallis' part, to exercise properly the required skills associated with interpersonal competency would have major repercussions in October 1781 and the outcome of the war.

8

THE YORKTOWN CAMPAIGN

Cornwallis spent most of April 1781 in Wilmington, N.C. letting his soldiers rest and get resupplied. During the late spring and most of the summer he moved his army into Virginia, hoping to carry out the strategy he and Lord Germain had devised. The heart of this strategy was to draw Washinton's army into Virginia and defeat it in a culminating battle of which Cornwallis was so fond.[42] In the meantime, Clinton was forced to accept the new strategy, but was personally obsessed with both an American/French attack on New York City (which was exactly what Washington had in mind), and ensuring that Cornwallis was responsive to Clinton's role as Commander-in-Chief.[43] Thus, during the summer, after minor inconsequential skirmishes along the way with American forces under the Marquis de Lafayette, Cornwallis arrived at Yorktown in early August 1781.[44]

It was at this point that Cornwallis engaged in another series of miscalculations in strategic thinking that would lead to his surrender at Yorktown. First, because of the superiority of the British navy, he assumed that his position on the Virginia coast would be safe. Second, he believed that because Lord Germain had agreed to the new southern strategy, that Clinton would fully support the plan and therefore substantially reinforce his position at Yorktown in time to meet any combined American/French threat. Finally, Cornwallis underestimated the Washington and Rochambeau's generalship.

Once established at Yorktown, Cornwallis began a slow but methodical buildup of fortifications in case of attack from the landward side.[45] When in early September a powerful French fleet, under the command of Admiral De Grasse, entered the Chesapeake Bay, Cornwallis was not perturbed. After all, "disaster at the hands of the Bourbons was all but incomprehensible to the British mind of the eighteenth century."[46] The unthinkable happened when De Grasse defeated a British squadron under Admiral Graves in the Battle of the Chesapeake Capes on September 5, 1781.[47] The outcome of this battle was that Cornwallis was now completely blockaded. Cornwallis is often criticized for not using his numerical superiority over Lafayette at this time to conduct a breakout and engagement. His decision to remain behind defenses at Yorktown is partly attributed to arrogance regarding the supposed superiority of the British navy, and partly because he had learned a lesson in the futility of chasing American forces around the country side in the Carolinas.[48] In this case his decision to remain behind the defenses at Yorktown resulted in a lost opportunity to deal the Americans a decisive defeat and thereby weaken Washington and Rochambeau's position when they arrived in mid September.

The correspondence between Clinton and Cornwallis, from his arrival at Yorktown to his surrender, was adversarial at best.[49] Clinton continuously criticized Cornwallis for getting bottled up on the Yorktown peninsula. Cornwallis firied back letters protesting the commander's criticisms "as unexpected, as, I trust, they are undeserved."[50] With Washington and Rochambeau on the way south to reinforce Lafayette, the Chesapeake Bay blockaded and Cornwallis and Clinton second-guessing each othe,r it would have been prudent for Cornwallis, as the subordinate officer, to rise above the pettiness for the good of the British cause. Instead, "the continuing squabble in the British high command did nothing to further the work in Yorktown."[51] As early as the 17 September, Cornwallis realized his position was becoming untenable and he wrote to Clinton, "This place is in no state of defence. If you cannot relieve me very soon, you must be prepared to hear the worst."[52] Clinton finally did decided to reinforce Cornwallis, but arrived at the Chesapeake Bay on 25 October - six days after Cornwallis had surrendered. Six days of delay might have been avoided if Cornwallis had taken the initiative to stop the bickering.

Cornwallis' final error in judgment at Yorktown was that he underestimated Washington and Rochambeau's generalship. "The cooperation between Washington, Rochambeau, de Grasse...and Lafayette in a difficult and complex undertaking was virtually unparalleled in the history of eighteenth-century warfare."[53] It was Rochambeau, in fact, who convinced Washington that it made better strategic sense to attack Cornwallis at Yorktown with the aid of the French fleet in Chesapeake Bay rather than attack the firmly entrenched Clinton in New York.[54] From late September through mid October, combined American/French troops conducted siege operations against Cornwallis which included nearly continuous, heavy bombardment using French siege guns.[55]

During this period some of the arrogance and disdain Cornwallis held for his foe's abilities underwent a change. In an Initial letter to Clinton, he boasted, "I have ventured these last two days to look at General Washington's whole force in the position outside my works, and I have the pleasure to assure your Excellency that there was but one wish throughout the whole Army, which was, that the enemy would advance."[56] Four days before final surrender, Cornwallis' respect for his enemy had grown immeasurably. In a letter to Clinton on the 15 October, 1781, he writes, "the safety of the place is therefore so precarious that I cannot recommend that the fleet and army should run great risque in endeavoring to save us."[57] An uncharacteristic despair had engulfed Cornwallis at this point. Quite possibly it affected his ability to envision the opportunity to engage and defeat the American army, had he only held on until relief from Clinton arrived.

Cornwallis' actions at Yorktown directly led to his defeat. His over reliance on the superiority of the British navy, his constant bickering with his Commander-in-Chief and his underestimation of the abilities of his antagonists all were major factors in his loss at Yorktown. Other events played a part as well, but the ones listed above were all within his sphere of influence - if he had thought and acted as a strategic leader. There can be no doubt that his failure to integrate the conceptual, technical and interpersonal skills was largely responsible for the defeat at Yorktown and the loss of the American colonies to the British Empire. Yorktown did teach him valuable lessons for his future as a practitioner of the strategic leadership competencies however as, "America was the preface and the training ground for the glory that Cornwallis was to gain later in his military exploits in India."[58]

CORNWALLIS' CAREER AFTER YORKTOWN

"Just as the battle at Saratoga had been refought in the press for three years, so now Englishmen would read and discuss why defeat had been inflicted upon their army's most competent commander. Scores of official and semiofficial inquiries were forthcoming, and both Clinton and Cornwallis received a full hearing in the press. But the editors did not change their earlier position: Sir Henry was to blame."[59]

Although Cornwallis returned home to England as somewhat of a conquering hero the first few years were marred by a public squabble with Clinton over who was responsible for the Yorktown disaster. In the eyes of the king and the British public Cornwallis was absolved of blame associated with the loss of the war. King George gave him his personal "assurances that he did not hold Cornwallis to blame for the military disasters in America."[60] This hero worship of Cornwallis may seem misplaced at first analysis, but in the view of the subjects of British Empire in comparing Sir Henry Clinton's indecisive approach to war with that of Cornwallis', "the slow cautious approach is seldom appreciated by the general public, whereas all the world loves a fighter, especially one who came very close to winning."[61] While Sir Henry spent the rest of his life trying to defend his actions, "the general who actually surrendered at Yorktown was met with sympathy and a feeling that if he had been in overall command the outcome of the war could have been vastly different."[62] Thus Cornwallis found himself in a position to advance his skills as a strategic leader, and he made the most of it throughout the rest of his career.

In the summer of 1785, Cornwallis was chosen as the British Envoy to the court of Frederick the Great of Prussia. The stated purpose of this mission was to attend Prussian military reviews as the king's representative. Secretly, however, Cornwallis was directed to enter into negotiations with Prussia to form a military alliance with Great Britain. Although this particular alliance did not come to fruition Cornwallis became acquainted with the art of diplomacy, which would serve him well in future assignments.[63]

In 1786, Cornwallis accepted the politically and militarily demanding post of Governor General of India where he introduced a series of legal and administrative reforms known as the Cornwallis Code (1793). These reforms ensured that civil servants were adequately paid while at the same time forbidding them to engage in private business. Through this action Cornwallis established a tradition of law-abiding, incorruptible British rule in India. He also proved he had learned some valuable lessons in America when he effectively put down a rebellion, during the third of four Mysore Wars, by Sultan Tippoo Sahib against the Rajah of Travancore, an ally of the King. During this campaign, Cornwallis personally led British forces to victory, gaining significant additional holdings in India for England. For his services in India Cornwallis was promoted to full general and created a marquis.[64]

Cornwallis was appointed to the office of Master-General of Ordnance and given a seat in the king's cabinet. In this position he addressed some of the problems of the British military pension system, kept the British army well provisioned with arms and ammunition, and instituted long overdue humanitarian reforms throughout the service.[65]

In 1798, the grateful British government sent Cornwallis to Ireland to address yet another rebellion brewing there. As Viceroy of Ireland (1798-1801), he served with restraint and diplomacy. After suppressing the rebellion of Wolfe Tone in 1798 and defeating a French invasion force in the same year, he shrewdly insisted that only the revolutionary leaders be punished. Continuing to profit from lessons learned in India, Cornwallis worked to eliminate corruption among British officials in Ireland. He also supported the parliamentary union of Great Britain and Ireland and the concession of political rights to Roman Catholics. When King George III rejected these rights in 1801, Cornwallis resigned as Viceroy.[66]

Cornwallis was then chosen as the British representative to negotiate the Anglo-French peace Treaty of Amiens in March of 1802. This treaty, essentially negotiated between Cornwallis and Napoleon's brother Joseph, ended one phase of the Napoleonic wars. As a result of Cornwallis' developing negotiation skills England was at peace on the continent for the first time in nearly fifteen years.[67]

At the age of sixty-seven Cornwallis was again asked to serve in India. This time he was to put an end to warfare among rival native factions. He had hardly begun the task when he was stricken by fever, dying on October 5, 1805.[68]

Cornwallis' career from surrender at Yorktown to his death in 1805 is proof that the strategic leadership competencies are skills that are learned over time, often through trial and error. His story is one of a gifted operational commander who learned about the value of developing the conceptual, technical, and interpersonal competencies to complement his innate virtues of high moral standards, an acute sense of honor, and selfless devotion to duty while serving his country. During this timeframe very few strategic leaders anywhere on the globe can match Cornwallis' record as a practitioner of the strategic leadership competencies in carrying out the military and policy objectives of the British Empire.

History's assessment of Lord Cornwallis as a military commander and strategic leader is further substantiation that he became an adroit practitioner of the strategic leadership competencies. An 1832 British publication commenting on British commanders to that time states:

> "Now an officer, who is never more at home than on a field of battle, or in front of an enemies town, - who is master of manoeuvre, a skillful leader both in advance and retreat, and familiarly acquainted with the capabilities of all under his command, - cannot even, though wanting in other and not less essential points, be accounted a mean man in the list of military commanders. To Marlborough, to Peterborough, or even to Wolfe, we should certainly not compare him, but the Marquis Cornwallis is a name of which the British army has no cause to be ashamed."[69]

A more recent American assessment of the Earl as a strategic leader and policy maker gives the reader insight into his ability to develop as a strategic leader over the breadth of his career:

> "During his long career of public service in the eighteenth and early nineteenth centuries, the first Marquis Cornwallis helped influence the course of history on three continents. His surrender at Yorktown occasioned the end of the American Revolution and ensured the triumph of American independence. His tenure as governor general and commander in chief in India represented a new phase in the history of British government there. He radically altered the traditional system of land tenure in Bengal and introduced some of the better elements of the English common law into the Bengal legal system. He reformed the civil service of India, imbuing it with an esprit de corps that fostered honesty and efficiency. Not least important, he fought a successful war against the Sultan of Mysore, thus adding substantially to the territories controlled by the East India Company. Several years later he served as governor general and commander in chief in Ireland, playing an important role in the events which led to the legislative union with Great Britain. Finally, his single venture into the labyrinth of European diplomacy resulted in the only period of peace his country knew during its twenty-year struggle against the imperial pretensions of France."[70]

CONCLUSION

This paper has shown that Lord Charles Cornwallis' failure to exercise the competencies of a strategic leader while in command of British forces at Yorktown in October 1781, effectively ended the American Revolutionary War and lost the American colonies to the British Empire.

His inability to synergize the conceptual, technical and interpersonal strategic skills resulted in a sub-optimal strategy in his prosecution of the war during the Carolinas and Yorktown campaigns. Cornwallis' conviction that major set battles would achieve British victory, arrogant belief in British naval invincibility, over-estimation of loyalist commitment, under-estimation of American leadership and partisan resolve, and inability to effectively interact with his Commander-in-Chief all contributed to his defeat at Yorktown. To be sure other factors played parts in the British defeat, but Cornwallis found himself immersed in one of those rare moments in history where his personal decisions made an unequivocal difference in global affairs, although he failed to realize the strategic importance of them at the time.

Why study the strategic failures and successes of Lord Cornwallis? What importance could the actions of an eighteenth century warrior/statesmen have to twenty first century strategic leaders? The relevance of this examination to future strategic leaders is that the flawed decisions of one man can unknowingly influence events that shape history. Cornwallis, although a superb tactical and operational commander, was simply not prepared at the Yorktown point in his career to anticipate the part his actions would take in the overall strategic outcome of the war. His failures provide future strategic leaders with an opportunity to learn from the mistakes of a man who would ultimately become one of the British Empire's military and political "superstars". Cornwallis' career after Yorktown is a litany of one global strategic success after another. The take away form this paper is that Cornwallis learned through experience, through trial and error, what it takes to be an outstanding practitioner of the strategic leader competencies - and so can today's developing leaders. Therefore, it is incumbent on future strategic leaders to become skilled practitioners of the strategic leader competencies as early as possible in their careers so that they can optimize decisions when thrown into the uncertain environments that characterize today's world.

WORD COUNT=6217

ENDNOTES

[1]Maurice Matloff, <u>American Military History</u> (Washington, D.C.: Office of the Chief of Military History, United States Army, 1969), 98.

[2]Thomas Deakin, "Vindication After Yorktown," <u>Military History</u>, April 1985, 10.

[3]Roderick R. Magee, II, Dr., ed., <u>Strategic Leadership Primer</u> (Department of Command, Leadership, and Management, United States Army War College, 1998), 3.

[4]Ibid., v.

[5]Ibid., 2.

[6]Ibid., 37.

[7]Ibid., 38-40.

[8]Ibid., 41.

[9]Ibid., 41-42.

[10]Ibid., 42-43.

[11]Franklin and Mary Wickwire, <u>Cornwallis: The American Adventure</u> (Boston: Houghton Mifflin Company, 1970), 29.

[12]Ibid., 7-16.

[13]Ibid., 17-29.

[14]Ibid., 30-46.

[15]George A. Billias, ed., <u>George Washington's Opponents: British Generals and Admirals in the American Revolution</u> (New York: William Morrow and Company Inc., 1969), 193.

[16]Magee, 37.

[17]William Seymour, <u>The Price of Glory: British Blunders in the War of American Independence</u> (London: Brassey's, 1995), 65-68.

[18]Wickwire, <u>Cornwallis: The American Adventure</u>, 85.

[19]Christopher Hibbert, <u>Redcoats and Rebels: The American Revolution Through British Eyes</u> (London: W.W. Norton and Company, 1990), 131.

[20]Billias, 197.

[21]Joseph B. Mitchell, <u>Military Leaders in the American Revolution</u> (McLean, VA: EPM Publications Inc., 1967), 177.

[22]Wickwire, <u>Cornwallis: The American Adventure</u>, 113.

[23]Billias, 197.

[24]Billias, 198.

[25]John M. Carroll and Colin F. Baxter, ed., <u>The American Military Tradition: From Colonial Times to the Present</u> (Wilmington, DE: Scholarly resources Inc., 1993), 11.

[26]Ibid.

[27]Hugh F. Rankin, <u>Greene and Cornwallis: The Campaign in the Carolinas</u> (Raleigh, NC: Department of Cultural Resources, Division of Archives and History, 1976), 27.

[28]Don Higginbotham, <u>The War of American Independence: Military Attitudes, Policies, and Practice, 1763-1789</u> (New York: The Macmillan Company, 1971), 357.

[29]Billias, 203.

[30]John Shy, <u>A People Numerous and Armed</u> (New York: Oxford University Press, 1976), 212-213.

[31]Seymour, 145-167.

[32]Higginbotham, 357-371.

[33]Donald Barr Chidsey, <u>The War in the South: An On the Scene Account of the Carolinas and Georgia in the American Revolution</u> (New York: Crown Publishers, 1957), 132.

[34]Hibbert, 274.

[35]Rankin, 80-83.

[36]Ibid., 83.

[37]Ibid.

[38]Brendan Morrissey, <u>Yorktown 1781: The World Turned Upside Down, Osprey Military Campaign Series</u> (Oxford, England: Osprey Publishing Ltd., 1999), 17.

[39]Hibbert, 316.

[40]Ibid., 317.

[41]Morrissey, 17.

[42]Higginbotham, 378.

[43]Hibbert, 315-320.

[44]Burke Davis, <u>The Campaign That Won America: The Story of Yorktown</u> (New York: The Dial Press, 1970), 111-127.

[45]Ibid., 134.

[46]Higginbotham, 381.

[47]Seymour, 217.

[48]Ibid., 219.

[49]Charles C. Cornwallis, <u>Correspondence of Charles, First Marquis Cornwallis</u>, Vol. 1, edited by Charles Ross. (London: Murray, 1859), 116-125.

[50]Davis, 133.

[51]Ibid.

[52]Cornwallis, 119.

[53]Higginbotham, 380.

[54]Marshall Count de Rochambeau, <u>Memoirs Relative to the War of Independence of the United States</u>, translated by M.W.E. Wright, Esq., (New York: The New York Times and Arno Press, 1971), 60-67.

[55]Davis, 213-237.

[56]Cornwallis, 120.

[57]Ibid., 124.

[58]Billias, 221.

[59]Solomon Lutnick, <u>The American Revolution and the British Press: 1775-1783</u> (Columbia, Missouri: University of Missouri Press, 1967), 189.

[60]Franklin and Mary Wickwire, <u>Cornwallis: The Imperial Years</u> (Chapel Hill, N.C.: The University of North Carolina Press, 1970), 7.

[61]Mitchell, 176.

[62]Ibid.

[63]Wickwire, <u>Cornwallis: The Imperial Years</u>, 16.

[64]Ibid., 19-154.

[65]Ibid., 206.

[66]Ibid., 208-252.

[67]Ibid., 255-262.

[68]Cornwallis, 16.

[69]G.R.Glieg, <u>Lives of the Most Eminent British Military Commanders</u> (London: Longman, Rees, Orme, Brown, Green, and John Taylor, 1831-1832), 195.

[70]Wickwire, <u>Cornwallis: The American Adventure</u>, 9.

BIBLIOGRAPHY

Billias, George A., ed. George Washington's Opponents: British Generals and Admirals in the American Revolution. New York: William Morrow and Company, Inc., 1969.

Carroll, John M., and Baxter, Colin F., ed. The American Military Tradition: From Colonial Times to the Present. Wilmington, DE: Scholarly Resources Inc., 1993.

Chidsey, Donald Barr. The War in the South: An On the Scene Account of the Carolinas and Georgia in the American Revolution. New York: Crown Publishers, 1957.

Cornwallis, Charles C. Correspondence of Charles, First Marquis Cornwallis. 3 Vols. Edited by Charles Ross. London: Murray,1859.

_____. An Answer to That Part of the Narrative of Lieutenant-General Sir Henry Clinton, K.B. Which Relates to the Conduct of Lieutenant-General Earl Cornwallis, During the Campaign in North-America, in the Year 1781. London: Debrett, 1783.

Dann, John C., ed. The Revolution Remembered: Eyewitness Accounts of the War for Independence. Chicago: The University of Chicago Press, 1980.

Davis, Burke. The Campaign That Won America: The Story of Yorktown. New York: The Dial Press, 1970.

Deakin, Thomas. "Vindication After Yorktown." Military History, April 1985, 10, 64-66.

Glieg, G.R. Lives of the Most Eminent British Military Commanders. London: Longman, Rees, Orme, Brown, Green, and John Taylor, 1831-1832.

Hibbert, Christopher. Redcoats and Rebels: The American Revolution Through British Eyes. London: W.W. Norton and Company, 1990.

Higginbotham, Don. The War of American Independence: Military Attitudes, Policies and Practice, 1763-1789. New York: The Macmillan Company, 1971.

Leckie, Robert. The Wars of America. New York: Harper and Row, 1981.

Lutnick, Solomon. The American Revolution and the British Press. Columbia, Missouri: University of Missouri Press, 1967.

Magee, Roderick R. II, Dr., ed. Strategic Leadership Primer. Department of Command, Leadership, and Management, United States Army War College, 1998.

Matloff, Maurice, ed. American Military History. Washington D.C.: Office of the Chief of Military History, United States Army, 1969.

Millet, Alan R., and Peter Maslowski. For the Common Defense: A Military History of the United States of America. New York: The Free Press, 1984.

Mitchell, Joseph B. Military Leaders in the American Revolution. McLean, VA: EPM Publications

Inc., 1967.

Morrissey, Brendan. Yorktown 1781: The World Turned Upside Down. Osprey Military Campaign Series: 47, Lee Johnson, ed. Oxford, England: Osprey Publishing Ltd., 1999.

Perret, Geoffrey. A Country Made By War: From the Revolution to Viet Nam - the Story of America's Rise to Power. New York: Random House, 1989.

Rankin, Hugh F. Greene and Cornwallis: The Campaign in the Carolinas. Raleigh, NC: Department of Cultural Resources, Division of Archives and History, 1976.

Rochambeau, Marshall Count de. Memoirs Relative to the War of Independence of the United States. Translated by M.W.E. Wright, Esq. New York: The New York Times and Arno Press, 1971.

Royster, Charles. A Revolutionary People at War: The Continental Army and American Character, 1775-1783. Chapel Hill: The University of North Carolina Press, 1979.

Scheer, George F., and Hugh F. Rankin. Rebels and Redcoats: The Living Story of the American Revolution. Cleveland: The World Publishing Company, 1957.

Seymour, William. The Price of Folley: British Blunders in the War of American Independence. London: Brassey's, 1995.

Shy, John. A People Numerous and Armed. New York: Oxford University Press, 1976.

Wickwire, Franklin and Mary. Cornwallis: The American Adventure. Boston: Houghton Mifflin Company, 1970.

_____. Cornwallis: The Imperial Years. Chapel Hill: The University of North Carolina Press, 1980.

Williams, Harry T. The History of American Wars From 1745-1918. New York: Alfred A. Knopf, 1981.

Wood, W.J. Battles of the Revolutionary War. Chapel Hill, N.C.: Algonquin Books of Chapel Hill, 1990.

Made in the USA
Middletown, DE
29 May 2022